ADDITION AND SUBTRACTION PRACTICE FOR 3RD GRADE

Math Books for Kids
Children's Math Books

Speedy Publishing LLC
40 E. Main St. #1156
Newark, DE 19711
www.speedypublishing.com

ADDITION

EXERCISE NO. 1

FIND THE SUM.

18 + 13	16 + 18	18 + 12	19 + 15
15 + 19	10 + 11	15 + 18	13 + 12
10 + 17	14 + 16	11 + 20	12 + 15

EXERCISE NO. 2

FIND THE SUM.

$$\begin{array}{r} 13 \\ +\,17 \\ \hline \end{array} \quad \begin{array}{r} 14 \\ +\,18 \\ \hline \end{array} \quad \begin{array}{r} 13 \\ +\,10 \\ \hline \end{array} \quad \begin{array}{r} 15 \\ +\,16 \\ \hline \end{array}$$

$$\begin{array}{r} 17 \\ +\,12 \\ \hline \end{array} \quad \begin{array}{r} 12 \\ +\,13 \\ \hline \end{array} \quad \begin{array}{r} 16 \\ +\,11 \\ \hline \end{array} \quad \begin{array}{r} 18 \\ +\,19 \\ \hline \end{array}$$

$$\begin{array}{r} 10 \\ +\,14 \\ \hline \end{array} \quad \begin{array}{r} 15 \\ +\,20 \\ \hline \end{array} \quad \begin{array}{r} 19 \\ +\,13 \\ \hline \end{array} \quad \begin{array}{r} 12 \\ +\,15 \\ \hline \end{array}$$

EXERCISE NO. 3

FIND THE SUM.

15 + 14	20 + 17	10 + 18	20 + 18
19 + 15	19 + 12	17 + 13	15 + 15
17 + 19	11 + 10	10 + 14	14 + 17

EXERCISE NO. 4

FIND THE SUM.

16 + 19	17 + 12	18 + 15	18 + 16
15 + 13	17 + 20	13 + 17	20 + 11
12 + 18	19 + 19	15 + 13	19 + 20

EXERCISE NO. 5

FIND THE SUM.

$$\begin{array}{r} 13 \\ +\,12 \\ \hline \end{array} \quad \begin{array}{r} 19 \\ +\,15 \\ \hline \end{array} \quad \begin{array}{r} 17 \\ +\,13 \\ \hline \end{array} \quad \begin{array}{r} 15 \\ +\,13 \\ \hline \end{array}$$

$$\begin{array}{r} 17 \\ +\,10 \\ \hline \end{array} \quad \begin{array}{r} 11 \\ +\,18 \\ \hline \end{array} \quad \begin{array}{r} 11 \\ +\,16 \\ \hline \end{array} \quad \begin{array}{r} 10 \\ +\,11 \\ \hline \end{array}$$

$$\begin{array}{r} 16 \\ +\,17 \\ \hline \end{array} \quad \begin{array}{r} 18 \\ +\,15 \\ \hline \end{array} \quad \begin{array}{r} 14 \\ +\,18 \\ \hline \end{array} \quad \begin{array}{r} 19 \\ +\,12 \\ \hline \end{array}$$

EXERCISE NO. 6

FIND THE SUM.

85 + 22	92 + 34	59 + 43	33 + 30
43 + 48	80 + 44	45 + 10	72 + 27
98 + 18	93 + 28	17 + 23	12 + 31

EXERCISE NO. 7

FIND THE SUM.

57 + 44	70 + 26	22 + 49	71 + 41
68 + 30	10 + 47	27 + 28	78 + 12
98 + 18	91 + 20	62 + 22	90 + 48

EXERCISE NO. 8

FIND THE SUM.

$$\begin{array}{r} 60 \\ +\,45 \\ \hline \end{array} \qquad \begin{array}{r} 22 \\ +\,29 \\ \hline \end{array} \qquad \begin{array}{r} 85 \\ +\,47 \\ \hline \end{array} \qquad \begin{array}{r} 26 \\ +\,16 \\ \hline \end{array}$$

$$\begin{array}{r} 95 \\ +\,37 \\ \hline \end{array} \qquad \begin{array}{r} 5 \\ +\,31 \\ \hline \end{array} \qquad \begin{array}{r} 76 \\ +\,49 \\ \hline \end{array} \qquad \begin{array}{r} 74 \\ +\,23 \\ \hline \end{array}$$

$$\begin{array}{r} 32 \\ +\,40 \\ \hline \end{array} \qquad \begin{array}{r} 28 \\ +\,38 \\ \hline \end{array} \qquad \begin{array}{r} 99 \\ +\,24 \\ \hline \end{array} \qquad \begin{array}{r} 65 \\ +\,21 \\ \hline \end{array}$$

EXERCISE NO. 9

FIND THE SUM.

14 + 41	82 + 26	78 + 45	88 + 38
64 + 47	33 + 49	38 + 17	99 + 22
62 + 31	50 + 12	58 + 48	39 + 27

EXERCISE NO. 10

FIND THE SUM.

60 + 22	45 + 49	11 + 27	47 + 14
54 + 19	15 + 42	96 + 41	10 + 43
37 + 45	93 + 13	92 + 29	64 + 46

EXERCISE NO. 11

FIND THE SUM.

4 + 22	91 + 19	69 + 48	12 + 42
57 + 39	42 + 33	59 + 13	52 + 45
10 + 41	40 + 26	96 + 17	73 + 36

EXERCISE NO. 12

FIND THE SUM.

94 + 20	61 + 47	19 + 26	32 + 33
34 + 32	12 + 18	87 + 23	70 + 48
71 + 43	18 + 29	29 + 15	43 + 30

EXERCISE NO. 13

FIND THE SUM.

265 + 22	330 + 12	387 + 12	763 + 16
345 + 24	750 + 44	327 + 21	541 + 16
361 + 21	160 + 27	571 + 16	473 + 14

EXERCISE NO. 14

FIND THE SUM.

671 + 12	351 + 27	842 + 17	858 + 31
736 + 21	627 + 11	332 + 36	831 + 67
270 + 22	483 + 15	868 + 31	423 + 35

EXERCISE NO. 15

FIND THE SUM.

866 + 11	612 + 21	877 + 11	548 + 31
427 + 11	384 + 13	722 + 73	474 + 15
588 + 11	768 + 21	214 + 23	143 + 33

EXERCISE NO. 16

FIND THE SUM.

$$\begin{array}{r} 373 \\ +\ 22 \\ \hline \end{array} \qquad \begin{array}{r} 618 \\ +\ 41 \\ \hline \end{array} \qquad \begin{array}{r} 757 \\ +\ 41 \\ \hline \end{array} \qquad \begin{array}{r} 382 \\ +\ 17 \\ \hline \end{array}$$

$$\begin{array}{r} 177 \\ +\ 21 \\ \hline \end{array} \qquad \begin{array}{r} 472 \\ +\ 11 \\ \hline \end{array} \qquad \begin{array}{r} 575 \\ +\ 22 \\ \hline \end{array} \qquad \begin{array}{r} 352 \\ +\ 35 \\ \hline \end{array}$$

$$\begin{array}{r} 516 \\ +\ 21 \\ \hline \end{array} \qquad \begin{array}{r} 835 \\ +\ 33 \\ \hline \end{array} \qquad \begin{array}{r} 640 \\ +\ 37 \\ \hline \end{array} \qquad \begin{array}{r} 613 \\ +\ 36 \\ \hline \end{array}$$

EXERCISE NO. 17

FIND THE SUM.

625 + 36	564 + 73	663 + 84	180 + 36
565 + 53	160 + 64	900 + 96	103 + 43
438 + 20	436 + 53	628 + 59	180 + 11

EXERCISE NO. 18

FIND THE SUM.

672 + 311	117 + 251	477 + 422	125 + 452
341 + 136	468 + 221	888 + 111	555 + 414
227 + 161	347 + 211	862 + 123	417 + 332

EXERCISE NO. 19

FIND THE SUM.

464 + 213	754 + 135	673 + 114	518 + 421
264 + 411	237 + 632	226 + 721	867 + 121
678 + 321	183 + 412	775 + 213	355 + 233

EXERCISE NO. 20

FIND THE SUM.

137 + 111	148 + 231	717 + 181	858 + 141
277 + 222	634 + 133	812 + 121	281 + 616
847 + 142	125 + 723	143 + 213	643 + 255

EXERCISE NO. 21

FIND THE SUM.

278 + 511	553 + 313	731 + 117	771 + 114
181 + 615	126 + 263	628 + 271	764 + 115
835 + 112	816 + 171	773 + 124	653 + 115

EXERCISE NO. 22

FIND THE SUM.

885 + 113	856 + 143	233 + 753	387 + 411
136 + 353	612 + 126	234 + 112	843 + 126
126 + 223	825 + 131	875 + 124	536 + 353

SUBTRACTION

EXERCISE NO. 23

FIND THE DIFFERENCE.

18 − 7	20 − 16	15 − 9	18 − 16
13 − 13	20 − 5	10 − 10	11 − 11
12 − 12	20 − 13	17 − 11	17 − 14

EXERCISE NO. 24

FIND THE DIFFERENCE.

$$\begin{array}{r} 16 \\ -\ 15 \\ \hline \end{array} \quad \begin{array}{r} 18 \\ -\ 13 \\ \hline \end{array} \quad \begin{array}{r} 17 \\ -\ 11 \\ \hline \end{array} \quad \begin{array}{r} 17 \\ -\ 17 \\ \hline \end{array}$$

$$\begin{array}{r} 16 \\ -\ 13 \\ \hline \end{array} \quad \begin{array}{r} 10 \\ -\ 7 \\ \hline \end{array} \quad \begin{array}{r} 12 \\ -\ 6 \\ \hline \end{array} \quad \begin{array}{r} 19 \\ -\ 10 \\ \hline \end{array}$$

$$\begin{array}{r} 14 \\ -\ 13 \\ \hline \end{array} \quad \begin{array}{r} 15 \\ -\ 14 \\ \hline \end{array} \quad \begin{array}{r} 19 \\ -\ 5 \\ \hline \end{array} \quad \begin{array}{r} 12 \\ -\ 9 \\ \hline \end{array}$$

EXERCISE NO. 25

FIND THE DIFFERENCE.

11 − 5 = ___	16 − 9 = ___	19 − 10 = ___	20 − 8 = ___
14 − 13 = ___	17 − 11 = ___	16 − 16 = ___	19 − 19 = ___
17 − 15 = ___	13 − 13 = ___	20 − 12 = ___	18 − 18 = ___

EXERCISE NO. 26

FIND THE DIFFERENCE.

12 - 9	13 - 5	16 - 11	17 - 14
19 - 15	11 - 6	13 - 11	12 - 7
18 - 12	18 - 14	16 - 10	20 - 15

EXERCISE NO. 27

FIND THE DIFFERENCE.

14 - 11	15 - 12	16 - 9	20 - 10
14 - 11	16 - 7	19 - 16	13 - 8
17 - 14	13 - 10	18 - 15	17 - 5

EXERCISE NO. 28

FIND THE DIFFERENCE.

$$\begin{array}{r} 81 \\ -\ 19 \\ \hline \end{array} \qquad \begin{array}{r} 46 \\ -\ 37 \\ \hline \end{array} \qquad \begin{array}{r} 90 \\ -\ 40 \\ \hline \end{array} \qquad \begin{array}{r} 91 \\ -\ 15 \\ \hline \end{array}$$

$$\begin{array}{r} 32 \\ -\ 13 \\ \hline \end{array} \qquad \begin{array}{r} 31 \\ -\ 23 \\ \hline \end{array} \qquad \begin{array}{r} 77 \\ -\ 20 \\ \hline \end{array} \qquad \begin{array}{r} 32 \\ -\ 26 \\ \hline \end{array}$$

$$\begin{array}{r} 53 \\ -\ 22 \\ \hline \end{array} \qquad \begin{array}{r} 56 \\ -\ 21 \\ \hline \end{array} \qquad \begin{array}{r} 72 \\ -\ 28 \\ \hline \end{array} \qquad \begin{array}{r} 68 \\ -\ 45 \\ \hline \end{array}$$

EXERCISE NO. 29

FIND THE DIFFERENCE.

$$\begin{array}{r} 57 \\ -\ 22 \\ \hline \end{array} \qquad \begin{array}{r} 78 \\ -\ 37 \\ \hline \end{array} \qquad \begin{array}{r} 96 \\ -\ 58 \\ \hline \end{array} \qquad \begin{array}{r} 90 \\ -\ 57 \\ \hline \end{array}$$

$$\begin{array}{r} 63 \\ -\ 36 \\ \hline \end{array} \qquad \begin{array}{r} 72 \\ -\ 50 \\ \hline \end{array} \qquad \begin{array}{r} 41 \\ -\ 25 \\ \hline \end{array} \qquad \begin{array}{r} 22 \\ -\ 19 \\ \hline \end{array}$$

$$\begin{array}{r} 73 \\ -\ 12 \\ \hline \end{array} \qquad \begin{array}{r} 38 \\ -\ 28 \\ \hline \end{array} \qquad \begin{array}{r} 91 \\ -\ 27 \\ \hline \end{array} \qquad \begin{array}{r} 33 \\ -\ 32 \\ \hline \end{array}$$

EXERCISE NO. 30

FIND THE DIFFERENCE.

59 - 19	69 - 50	38 - 32	89 - 49
91 - 15	55 - 21	94 - 45	95 - 27
62 - 18	78 - 51	50 - 14	80 - 25

EXERCISE NO. 31

FIND THE DIFFERENCE.

33 - 21	62 - 10	25 - 24	72 - 18
90 - 34	43 - 27	37 - 16	46 - 20
58 - 26	98 - 28	69 - 17	60 - 37

EXERCISE NO. 32

FIND THE DIFFERENCE.

$$\begin{array}{r} 91 \\ -\ 27 \\ \hline \end{array} \quad \begin{array}{r} 33 \\ -\ 23 \\ \hline \end{array} \quad \begin{array}{r} 93 \\ -\ 14 \\ \hline \end{array} \quad \begin{array}{r} 58 \\ -\ 28 \\ \hline \end{array}$$

$$\begin{array}{r} 48 \\ -\ 31 \\ \hline \end{array} \quad \begin{array}{r} 27 \\ -\ 10 \\ \hline \end{array} \quad \begin{array}{r} 31 \\ -\ 26 \\ \hline \end{array} \quad \begin{array}{r} 51 \\ -\ 22 \\ \hline \end{array}$$

$$\begin{array}{r} 25 \\ -\ 24 \\ \hline \end{array} \quad \begin{array}{r} 53 \\ -\ 53 \\ \hline \end{array} \quad \begin{array}{r} 47 \\ -\ 20 \\ \hline \end{array} \quad \begin{array}{r} 50 \\ -\ 28 \\ \hline \end{array}$$

EXERCISE NO. 33

FIND THE DIFFERENCE.

$$\begin{array}{r} 651 \\ -\ \ 77 \\ \hline \end{array} \quad \begin{array}{r} 236 \\ -\ \ 70 \\ \hline \end{array} \quad \begin{array}{r} 869 \\ -\ \ 74 \\ \hline \end{array} \quad \begin{array}{r} 967 \\ -\ \ 60 \\ \hline \end{array}$$

$$\begin{array}{r} 508 \\ -\ \ 80 \\ \hline \end{array} \quad \begin{array}{r} 230 \\ -\ \ 50 \\ \hline \end{array} \quad \begin{array}{r} 883 \\ -\ \ 62 \\ \hline \end{array} \quad \begin{array}{r} 726 \\ -\ \ 94 \\ \hline \end{array}$$

$$\begin{array}{r} 598 \\ -\ \ 83 \\ \hline \end{array} \quad \begin{array}{r} 527 \\ -\ \ 29 \\ \hline \end{array} \quad \begin{array}{r} 968 \\ -\ \ 70 \\ \hline \end{array} \quad \begin{array}{r} 930 \\ -\ \ 78 \\ \hline \end{array}$$

EXERCISE NO. 34

FIND THE DIFFERENCE.

527 - 38	234 - 41	510 - 41	500 - 45
565 - 56	904 - 38	932 - 38	892 - 70
385 - 31	723 - 99	810 - 75	810 - 76

EXERCISE NO. 35

FIND THE DIFFERENCE.

313 - 84	925 - 22	856 - 68	677 - 81
785 - 21	401 - 51	227 - 31	772 - 43
697 - 34	716 - 53	518 - 51	690 - 41

EXERCISE NO. 36

FIND THE DIFFERENCE.

235 - 72	277 - 11	608 - 86	343 - 81
639 - 99	373 - 66	645 - 62	318 - 88
224 - 66	426 - 94	876 - 36	538 - 11

EXERCISE NO. 37

FIND THE DIFFERENCE.

594 - 84	794 - 42	893 - 13	877 - 21
283 - 39	469 - 50	294 - 29	281 - 42
626 - 39	836 - 54	567 - 31	981 - 66

EXERCISE NO. 38

FIND THE DIFFERENCE.

494 - 60	774 - 18	339 - 65	629 - 56
336 - 76	536 - 61	656 - 92	594 - 13
450 - 22	553 - 24	373 - 59	973 - 64

EXERCISE NO. 39

FIND THE DIFFERENCE.

592 - 52	551 - 96	446 - 93	582 - 38
256 - 52	836 - 22	254 - 74	753 - 63
224 - 49	796 - 41	572 - 49	912 - 54

EXERCISE NO. 40

FIND THE DIFFERENCE.

555 - 132	975 - 234	667 - 151	859 - 645
558 - 341	566 - 132	657 - 235	899 - 522
858 - 326	765 - 342	676 - 314	798 - 515

EXERCISE NO. 41

FIND THE DIFFERENCE.

755 - 621	779 - 654	988 - 663	985 - 211
558 - 331	855 - 243	959 - 218	776 - 465
867 - 735	979 - 848	759 - 648	659 - 412

EXERCISE NO. 42

FIND THE DIFFERENCE.

897 - 173	988 - 466	888 - 163	685 - 113
565 - 241	787 - 455	568 - 426	565 - 424
759 - 127	686 - 445	775 - 451	687 - 513

EXERCISE NO. 43

FIND THE DIFFERENCE.

788 - 646	599 - 243	996 - 383	988 - 863
678 - 127	887 - 536	979 - 721	786 - 245
877 - 344	665 - 233	686 - 262	777 - 561

EXERCISE NO. 44

FIND THE DIFFERENCE.

876 - 552	967 - 212	686 - 512	986 - 152
569 - 217	696 - 553	955 - 744	577 - 336
765 - 211	587 - 444	868 - 457	798 - 484

GOOD JOB!

ANSWERS!

EXERCISE NO. 1

18 + 13 31	16 + 18 34	18 + 12 30	19 + 15 34
15 + 19 34	10 + 11 21	15 + 18 33	13 + 12 25
10 + 17 27	14 + 16 30	11 + 20 31	12 + 15 27

EXERCISE NO. 2

13 + 17 30	14 + 18 32	13 + 10 23	15 + 16 31
17 + 12 29	12 + 13 25	16 + 11 27	18 + 19 37
10 + 14 24	15 + 20 35	19 + 13 32	12 + 15 27

EXERCISE NO. 3

15 + 14 29	20 + 17 37	10 + 18 28	20 + 18 38
19 + 15 34	19 + 12 31	17 + 13 30	15 + 15 30
17 + 19 36	11 + 10 21	10 + 14 24	14 + 17 31

EXERCISE NO. 4

16 + 19 35	17 + 12 29	18 + 15 33	18 + 16 34
15 + 13 28	17 + 20 37	13 + 17 30	20 + 11 31
12 + 18 30	19 + 19 38	15 + 13 28	19 + 20 39

EXERCISE NO. 5

13	19	17	15
+ 12	+ 15	+ 13	+ 13
25	34	30	28
17	11	11	10
+ 10	+ 18	+ 16	+ 11
27	29	27	21
16	18	14	19
+ 17	+ 15	+ 18	+ 12
33	33	32	31

EXERCISE NO. 6

85	92	59	33
+ 22	+ 34	+ 43	+ 30
107	126	102	63
43	80	45	72
+ 48	+ 44	+ 10	+ 27
91	124	55	99
98	93	17	12
+ 18	+ 28	+ 23	+ 31
116	121	40	43

EXERCISE NO. 7

57	70	22	71
+ 44	+ 26	+ 49	+ 41
101	96	71	112
68	10	27	78
+ 30	+ 47	+ 28	+ 12
98	57	55	90
98	91	62	90
+ 18	+ 20	+ 22	+ 48
116	111	84	138

EXERCISE NO. 8

60	22	85	26
+ 45	+ 29	+ 47	+ 16
105	51	132	42
95	5	76	74
+ 37	+ 31	+ 49	+ 23
132	36	125	97
32	28	99	65
+ 40	+ 38	+ 24	+ 21
72	66	123	86

EXERCISE NO. 9

14 + 41 55	82 + 26 108	78 + 45 123	88 + 38 126
64 + 47 111	33 + 49 82	38 + 17 55	99 + 22 121
62 + 31 93	50 + 12 62	58 + 48 106	39 + 27 66

EXERCISE NO. 10

60 + 22 82	45 + 49 94	11 + 27 38	47 + 14 61
54 + 19 73	15 + 42 57	96 + 41 137	10 + 43 53
37 + 45 82	93 + 13 106	92 + 29 121	64 + 46 110

EXERCISE NO. 11

4 + 22 26	91 + 19 110	69 + 48 117	12 + 42 54
57 + 39 96	42 + 33 75	59 + 13 72	52 + 45 97
10 + 41 51	40 + 26 66	96 + 17 113	73 + 36 109

EXERCISE NO. 12

94 + 20 114	61 + 47 108	19 + 26 45	32 + 33 65
34 + 32 66	12 + 18 30	87 + 23 110	70 + 48 118
71 + 43 114	18 + 29 47	29 + 15 44	43 + 30 73

EXERCISE NO. 13

265	330	387	763
+ 22	+ 12	+ 12	+ 16
287	342	399	779
345	750	327	541
+ 24	+ 44	+ 21	+ 16
369	794	348	557
361	160	571	473
+ 21	+ 27	+ 16	+ 14
382	187	587	487

EXERCISE NO. 14

671	351	842	858
+ 12	+ 27	+ 17	+ 31
683	378	859	889
736	627	332	831
+ 21	+ 11	+ 36	+ 67
757	638	368	898
270	483	868	423
+ 22	+ 15	+ 31	+ 35
292	498	899	458

EXERCISE NO. 15

866	612	877	548
+ 11	+ 21	+ 11	+ 31
877	633	888	579
427	384	722	474
+ 11	+ 13	+ 73	+ 15
438	397	795	489
588	768	214	143
+ 11	+ 21	+ 23	+ 33
599	789	237	176

EXERCISE NO. 16

373	618	757	382
+ 22	+ 41	+ 41	+ 17
395	659	798	399
177	472	575	352
+ 21	+ 11	+ 22	+ 35
198	483	597	387
516	835	640	613
+ 21	+ 33	+ 37	+ 36
537	868	677	649

EXERCISE NO. 17

625	564	663	180
+ 36	+ 73	+ 84	+ 36
661	637	747	216
565	160	900	103
+ 53	+ 64	+ 96	+ 43
618	224	996	146
438	436	628	180
+ 20	+ 53	+ 59	+ 11
458	489	687	191

EXERCISE NO. 18

672	117	477	125
+ 311	+ 251	+ 422	+ 452
983	368	899	577
341	468	888	555
+ 136	+ 221	+ 111	+ 414
477	689	999	969
227	347	862	417
+ 161	+ 211	+ 123	+ 332
388	558	985	749

EXERCISE NO. 19

464	754	673	518
+ 213	+ 135	+ 114	+ 421
677	889	787	939
264	237	226	867
+ 411	+ 632	+ 721	+ 121
675	869	947	988
678	183	775	355
+ 321	+ 412	+ 213	+ 233
999	595	988	588

EXERCISE NO. 20

137	148	717	858
+ 111	+ 231	+ 181	+ 141
248	379	898	999
277	634	812	281
+ 222	+ 133	+ 121	+ 616
499	767	933	897
847	125	143	643
+ 142	+ 723	+ 213	+ 255
989	848	356	898

EXERCISE NO. 21

278 + 511 789	553 + 313 866	731 + 117 848	771 + 114 885
181 + 615 796	126 + 263 389	628 + 271 899	764 + 115 879
835 + 112 947	816 + 171 987	773 + 124 897	653 + 115 768

EXERCISE NO. 22

885 + 113 998	856 + 143 999	233 + 753 986	387 + 411 798
136 + 353 489	612 + 126 738	234 + 112 346	843 + 126 969
126 + 223 349	825 + 131 956	875 + 124 999	536 + 353 889

EXERCISE NO. 23

18 - 7 11	20 - 16 4	15 - 9 6	18 - 16 2
13 - 13 0	20 - 5 15	10 - 10 0	11 - 11 0
12 - 12 0	20 - 13 7	17 - 11 6	17 - 14 3

EXERCISE NO. 24

16 - 15 1	18 - 13 5	17 - 11 6	17 - 17 0
16 - 13 3	10 - 7 3	12 - 6 6	19 - 10 9
14 - 13 1	15 - 14 1	19 - 5 14	12 - 9 3

EXERCISE NO. 25

11	16	19	20
- 5	- 9	- 10	- 8
6	7	9	12
14	17	16	19
- 13	- 11	- 16	- 19
1	6	0	0
17	13	20	18
- 15	- 13	- 12	- 18
2	0	8	0

EXERCISE NO. 26

12	13	16	17
- 9	- 5	- 11	- 14
3	8	5	3
19	11	13	12
- 15	- 6	- 11	- 7
4	5	2	5
18	18	16	20
- 12	- 14	- 10	- 15
6	4	6	5

EXERCISE NO. 27

14	15	16	20
- 11	- 12	- 9	- 10
3	3	7	10
14	16	19	13
- 11	- 7	- 16	- 8
3	9	3	5
17	13	18	17
- 14	- 10	- 15	- 5
3	3	3	12

EXERCISE NO. 28

81	46	90	91
- 19	- 37	- 40	- 15
62	9	50	76
32	31	77	32
- 13	- 23	- 20	- 26
19	8	57	6
53	56	72	68
- 22	- 21	- 28	- 45
31	35	44	23

EXERCISE NO. 29

57	78	96	90
- 22	- 37	- 58	- 57
35	41	38	33
63	72	41	22
- 36	- 50	- 25	- 19
27	22	16	3
73	38	91	33
- 12	- 28	- 27	- 32
61	10	64	1

EXERCISE NO. 30

59	69	38	89
- 19	- 50	- 32	- 49
40	19	6	40
91	55	94	95
- 15	- 21	- 45	- 27
76	34	49	68
62	78	50	80
- 18	- 51	- 14	- 25
44	27	36	55

EXERCISE NO. 31

33	62	25	72
- 21	- 10	- 24	- 18
12	52	1	54
90	43	37	46
- 34	- 27	- 16	- 20
56	16	21	26
58	98	69	60
- 26	- 28	- 17	- 37
32	70	52	23

EXERCISE NO. 32

91	33	93	58
- 27	- 23	- 14	- 28
64	10	79	30
48	27	31	51
- 31	- 10	- 26	- 22
17	17	5	29
25	53	47	50
- 24	- 53	- 20	- 28
1	0	27	22

EXERCISE NO. 33

651 - 77 574	236 - 70 166	869 - 74 795	967 - 60 907
508 - 80 428	230 - 50 180	883 - 62 821	726 - 94 632
598 - 83 515	527 - 29 498	968 - 70 898	930 - 78 852

EXERCISE NO. 34

527 - 38 489	234 - 41 193	510 - 41 469	500 - 45 455
565 - 56 509	904 - 38 866	932 - 38 894	892 - 70 822
385 - 31 354	723 - 99 624	810 - 75 735	810 - 76 734

EXERCISE NO. 35

313 - 84 229	925 - 22 903	856 - 68 788	677 - 81 596
785 - 21 764	401 - 51 350	227 - 31 196	772 - 43 729
697 - 34 663	716 - 53 663	518 - 51 467	690 - 41 649

EXERCISE NO. 36

235 - 72 163	277 - 11 266	608 - 86 522	343 - 81 262
639 - 99 540	373 - 66 307	645 - 62 583	318 - 88 230
224 - 66 158	426 - 94 332	876 - 36 840	538 - 11 527

EXERCISE NO. 37

594	794	893	877
- 84	- 42	- 13	- 21
510	752	880	856

283	469	294	281
- 39	- 50	- 29	- 42
244	419	265	239

626	836	567	981
- 39	- 54	- 31	- 66
587	782	536	915

EXERCISE NO. 38

494	774	339	629
- 60	- 18	- 65	- 56
434	756	274	573

336	536	656	594
- 76	- 61	- 92	- 13
260	475	564	581

450	553	373	973
- 22	- 24	- 59	- 64
428	529	314	909

EXERCISE NO. 39

592	551	446	582
- 52	- 96	- 93	- 38
540	455	353	544

256	836	254	753
- 52	- 22	- 74	- 63
204	814	180	690

224	796	572	912
- 49	- 41	- 49	- 54
175	755	523	858

EXERCISE NO. 40

555	975	667	859
- 132	- 234	- 151	- 645
423	741	516	214

558	566	657	899
- 341	- 132	- 235	- 522
217	434	422	377

858	765	676	798
- 326	- 342	- 314	- 515
532	423	362	283

EXERCISE NO. 41

755	779	988	985
- 621	- 654	- 663	- 211
134	125	325	774

558	855	959	776
- 331	- 243	- 218	- 465
227	612	741	311

867	979	759	659
- 735	- 848	- 648	- 412
132	131	111	247

EXERCISE NO. 42

897	988	888	685
- 173	- 466	- 163	- 113
724	522	725	572

565	787	568	565
- 241	- 455	- 426	- 424
324	332	142	141

759	686	775	687
- 127	- 445	- 451	- 513
632	241	324	174

EXERCISE NO. 43

788	599	996	988
- 646	- 243	- 383	- 863
142	356	613	125

678	887	979	786
- 127	- 536	- 721	- 245
551	351	258	541

877	665	686	777
- 344	- 233	- 262	- 561
533	432	424	216

EXERCISE NO. 44

876	967	686	986
- 552	- 212	- 512	- 152
324	755	174	834

569	696	955	577
- 217	- 553	- 744	- 336
352	143	211	241

765	587	868	798
- 211	- 444	- 457	- 484
554	143	411	314

Visit
BABY PROFESSOR
EDUCATION KIDS
www.BabyProfessorBooks.com
to download Free Baby Professor eBooks
and view our catalog of new and exciting
Children's Books

www.ingramcontent.com/pod-product-compliance
Lightning Source LLC
LaVergne TN
LVHW060826170826
845678LV00010B/1914
9798869441614